www.drtonymag.com

OBAMACARE

A Doctor's Guide to Saving Healthcare

Tony Maglione MD

createspace™

CreateSpace is a DBA of On-Demand Publishing LLC, part of the Amazon group of companies.

Printed in the United States of America

Copyright © 2011 by Tony Maglione
All rights reserved, including the right to reproduce this book or portions thereof in any form whatsoever.

Library of Congress Control Number: 2011904627

ISBN 1460965876
ISBN 978-1460965870

Dedicated to Hippocrates, who stated:

"I will prescribe regimens for the good of my patients according to my ability and my judgment…If I keep this oath faithfully, may I enjoy my life and practice my art, respected by all men and in all times; but if I swerve from it or violated it, may the reverse be my lot."

Acknowledgments

Tony Maglione would like to thank his wife, Mindy, for all her support and contributions. He also wishes to thank all his patients over the years of practicing medicine, for these patients are the ones that gave him the inspiration to write this book.

Contents

Introduction ....Page 1

Section I
Healthcare and Obamacare

Chapter 1
What Is Healthcare? ....Page 6

Chapter 2
What Is the Responsibility of the Patient ?..........Page 12

Chapter 3
What Is the Responsibility of the Doctor? ....Page 16

Chapter 4
What Is Right with Obamacare? ....Page 22

Chapter 5
What Is Wrong with Obamacare? ....Page 24

Chapter 6
What Is the Responsibility of Government? ....Page 50

Chapter 7
What Is the Track Record of Government's
Involvement in Healthcare? ....Page 52

Chapter 8
Is Increasing the Bureaucracy the Answer?.........Page 56

Section II
What are the Solutions?

Chapter 9
Insurance Across State Lines ....Page 63

Chapter 10
Tort Reform ....Page 68

Chapter 11
No Exclusions for Preexisting Conditions ....Page 74

Chapter 12
Cap for Catastrophic Care ....Page 78

Chapter 13
Entry Age for Medicare ....Page 80

Chapter 14
Medicare Coverage with Advancing Age ....Page 83

Chapter 15
Means Testing for Medicare Beneficiaries ....Page 87

Chapter 16
Health Savings Accounts ....Page 90

Chapter 17
Allow Medicare Advantage ....Page 92

Chapter 18
Health Insurance Exchange ....Page 94

Chapter 19
Medicaid – State Responsibility, Not Federal ....Page 96

Chapter 20
Tax Benefits for Health Insurance ....Page 97

Chapter 21
State Experiments ....Page 99

Chapter 22
Doctor Regulation ....Page 103

Chapter 23
Pharmaceutical Companies ....Page 106

Chapter 24
Immigration ....Page 108

Chapter 25
Reform Other Entitlements ....Page 112

Chapter 26
Funding for Abortion ....Page 119

Chapter 27
Education ....Page 121

Section III
Congress and the Presidency

Chapter 28
What is Congress' Role?..Page 124

Chapter 29
Winning Strategy ....Page 126

Conclusion ....Page 131

Sources..Page 136

Appendix ....Page 140

Introduction

Does Congress really understand healthcare in America? Do the members know how to improve it? As a fourth generation doctor, it was obvious to me that the 111th Congress (2009-2010) did not have a clue about how to reform the US healthcare system, which is considered the best in the world. Like many others in healthcare, I was very upset about the process by which Obamacare was passed in March 2010. Obamacare can be referred to as the *Healthcare Reconciliation Bill HR 4872* or *Patient Protection and Affordable Care Act* (which is a misnomer since it will eventually be unaffordable and, therefore, not very protective of patients). The very process by which it was passed, including trickery, bribery, and closed-door deliberations with no input from opposing points of view, demonstrates the mindset of the legislators. How can a mindset that operates in this way be trusted to come up with solutions for healthcare? Healthcare is not only responsible for one-sixth of our economy, but also has a personal, emotional effect on every individual American.

Because of the increasing cost of healthcare and increasing demands on the system due to the aging population, reform is necessary. The 111th Congress ended up completely transforming healthcare instead of improving it by controlling costs and maintaining the current, excellent quality of care. Their approach to solving problems is counterproductive and may be deadly for many Americans.

Any fair-minded or experienced healthcare provider, including doctors, nurse practitioners, and physician assistants, knows that government involvement is almost always intrusive and tends to complicate rather than simplify. The government's involvement is usually cost inefficient and results in waste and decreased quality of care in almost all circumstances.

The approach to solutions for the current problems or issues with healthcare needs to be a scientific and common sense approach utilizing sound financial principles and proven outcomes. Using a scientific approach is a way of ensuring better odds in solving or reaching a solution. The current Obamacare bill is based on ideology and not on a scientific approach and will negatively affect current healthcare by decreasing its quality and increasing mortality and morbidity.

The main purpose of this book is to educate the public and hopefully some politicians of the rationale behind the need to repeal Obamacare and then use some of its good points and rewrite solutions that will work and can be passed by Congress and signed by the president. Since President Obama will most likely not sign a law repealing Obamacare, it is incumbent upon the citizens of this country to vote for a new leader in the presidential election of 2012 so that the future of healthcare has the opportunity to remain solvent from both a fiscal point of view and in maintaining its excellent quality of care. If we do not vote for a new president, one who believes Obamacare has to be replaced, our healthcare system will not remain solvent within the next ten years, and these consequences will be deadly, both literally and financially. There is also a need to have solutions that are ready for legislative approval when the new president takes office in 2013. This book will offer solutions that will need to be incorporated in any new healthcare bill in order to give it the best chance for success. There are enough leaders in Congress, such as Senator Jim DeMint, Congressmen Eric Cantor, Paul Ryan, and John Boehner, and Congresswoman Michele Bachmann and others, who can achieve these goals. I will try to explain why allowing this healthcare bill to continue in its current form is not in

America's best interest for the present and future generations. In order for healthcare to remain solvent, the current Congress, and for that matter all future Congress members, will need to address other spending that affects the amount of funds available to healthcare. These include addressing the interest incurred by our national debt, Social Security expenses, and other entitlements and discretionary spending. If we do not address these issues responsibly in the very near future, the ability to remain a financially solvent and strong economic nation will have passed us by.

Section I

Healthcare and Obamacare

Chapter 1

What Is Healthcare?

Health is important to both the individual and the nation as a whole. For the individual, good health enables one to better fulfill the American ideals of liberty, freedom, and the pursuit of happiness. On a practical level, good health better enables one to take care of himself or herself and his/her family. For the nation, the better the health of its individual citizens, the more productive the citizens are, and the more prosperous the nation will be.

Healthcare in our country began as individuals caring for others, even before medical licensing. Healthcare was developed in our system by the private sector, and the method of payment was always established between the customer or patient and the provider or physician. The type and amount of payment changed throughout time, as we have all heard stories of payment for services with food, livestock, or other forms of bartering. Prior to the beginning of Medicare and Medicaid in the mid-1960s, administrative costs in a doctor's office were minimal. When a doctor took care of a poor or indigent patient who did not have any means to pay for his bill, the doctor did not even bother to write out a bill. During these times, every American was cared for in one way or another. Now, the indigent, or those without insurance, go to emergency rooms for their care. This is an unworkable long-term solution and is expensive for all Americans.

To understand how to improve and change healthcare for the better, one needs to understand the evolution of healthcare in our country over the last three hundred years. Since there has always been change throughout the history of medicine in America, we should not be afraid of instituting change now to enable a better future. The American medical past included several opposing entities such as government, conventional medicine, unconventional medicine, and science. Medicine was constantly being altered by struggles, compromises, and accommodations among citizens with conflicting views and interests. This is much like it is today, except today also includes unwelcome political factors in determining policies on healthcare.

In colonial times, during the 1700s, there was a conflict between government and the private sector. Government was under pressure to organize measures against epidemic diseases and to make provisions for healthcare for the poor and other special groups. Conflict between private medical interests and organizations forced the government to assume roles as regulators and protectors of public health interests. By the end of the 1900s, government overstepped these roles, and instead of regulators and protectors of the healthcare system, they grew to be more and more controlling of the healthcare system.

In the 1800s, urban dwellers enjoyed longer life expectancies because of sanitary services. These sanitary services were not available in rural areas where farmers and rural towns existed. These rural towns received limited benefits from medicine and became more self-sufficient. During the 1800s, practitioners increasingly became associated with main line therapies and organizations. By the late 1800s, science began to assume a major role, after realizing the importance of the laboratory and adoption of its scientific method.

In the next century, the 1900s, as the nation became richer in both rural areas and cities, the health expectations increased. For example, life expectancy has doubled over the last three hundred years. So government became more involved in health issues, sanitary services, and private and public healthcare institutions and personnel. Government then assumed further influence over education and medical research, hospitals, health finance corporations, medications, and foods, as well as other health matters. In the twentieth century, especially after World War II, there was increased use of surgery because of the discovery of anesthesia; and there was increased research and use of laboratories. This helped to evolve standards that increased quality of care. The number of medical schools increased and professionalism was created with a standard of credentialing, medical licensing, and education requirements. All of these changes were spurred on by the private sector, individual physicians, in order to validate the level of professionalism and increase the importance of the profession. For example, in the 1800s, doctors or teams of doctors made discoveries like small pox inoculation. Doctors or scientists today need incentives for further medical discoveries and innovations. This is enhanced by a free market, entrepreneurial spirit. Without this, America's international prominence in medicine will diminish significantly in the future.

As America became a superpower by the mid-1900s, because of its military and economic strength, American medicine also became the superpower internationally. America had achieved a medical prestige equal to its economic and military strength.

Initially, hospitals were a place where patients were sent for diagnosis, as well as to be treated. Eventually, with more scientific discoveries, diagnosis was accomplished for non-emergencies in the outpatient setting.

In the 1950s, there was an increase in the medical industrial community, which led to open heart surgery, organ transplantation, and high-cost technology such as the CT-scan and MRI. This led to rising costs with an increased percentage of healthcare costs to the national economy with each passing year. At the current time, healthcare comprises 16 percent of national spending. It is predicted that in 2020, it will account for more than 20 percent of the national economy. One of the problems that will need to be addressed in healthcare reform is that as healthcare grows its technology, it then becomes more costly and less affordable for Americans.

Is the American healthcare system really the best in the world? Some would argue that it is not because of certain statistics from the World Health Organization (WHO), such as infant mortality. The American healthcare system has the best technology in the world and it is where many people in the world come for their care. Americans are not seeking better care by going to other countries.

What type of healthcare do Americans really want in the future? Do we want Congress to define healthcare? Or do we as public citizens want to control the debate and define healthcare so that it applies to all Americans? Do we want Obamacare? Before examining what is right and what is wrong with Obamacare, one needs to understand the responsibilities of both the patient and the provider (doctor, nurse practitioner, or physician assistant).

Chapter 2

What Is the Responsibility of the Patient?

The patient is the consumer; this includes all Americans. The level of responsibility by the patient should remain the same regardless of what type of healthcare system is in place. The patient has the responsibility to become educated on behavior or habits that are unhealthy and more of a financial strain on healthcare. The government should not be in the business of deciding for individual citizens what is good for their health, but rather should help educate the public on why certain choices are unhealthy. The patient should have the choice and freedom to choose his/her behavior, however costly the behavior may be. But this patient should also expect to pay more into the system. For example, with a life insurance policy, if a person smokes, has high cholesterol, or participates in risky behavior such as sky diving, that person can expect to pay higher premiums for the same amount of life insurance coverage. The same applies for car insurance, where if a person is more accident-prone or has more speeding tickets, his car insurance premiums will be higher. The choice of behavior by the patient should not be restricted; that is, the patient should have the freedom to continue behavior or habits that are unhealthy and result in a higher likelihood of healthcare costs in the future. The government shouldn't restrict these choices, but patients should understand that these choices do lead to higher costs and, therefore, just like life or car insurance premiums are higher, those health insurance premiums should be higher in patients who have these behaviors.

We cannot continue to pay for certain behavior that is an individual's choice, such as smoking or drinking. As a society, it is absurd to think that this type of behavior should be rewarded by not paying higher premiums. This is just like when there were provisions in welfare back in the 1980s and early 1990s so that single unwed mothers would get more money by having more children and keeping the father out of the home. This strategy is counterproductive in that it hurts these children because of the dependency on government and the likelihood of becoming less educated. This leads to a cycle of less earning potential and a higher rate of social problems. It is well known that children from moms who are married have over a five times greater chance of having a college degree than those children reared by moms who are unwed. Someone with a college degree is known to have a higher average income than a high school graduate or high school dropout. In an effort to assist unwed single moms, the system of rewarding a mom by the number of children she has may have been well-intentioned, but ended up entrapping this population by creating an environment with less possibility for these moms to work, and keeping them dependent on government for their subsistence. When welfare evolved into a program of workfare in the mid-1990s instead of government dependency, a higher percentage of these people in poverty went into the middle-class, a decade later than at any other time in our history. This same philosophy of personal responsibility should be applied for healthcare since it is cost effective and more beneficial for the individual.

Patients need to know that certain choices they make that affect their health are more costly, and that they will need to pay for these choices with higher premiums. This will result in a gradual decrease in costly habits because there will be an economic incentive to change behavior.

Also, with respect to personal responsibility and choice, when the patient is a member of Congress, who passes laws that affect healthcare for all Americans, he or she should abide by the same regulations. When Congress passed the healthcare bill in 2010, the regulations did not apply to their healthcare since Congress has different health insurance coverage for their members and their families. This is a double standard that should make all Americans distrust any politician that is unwilling to live by the very laws that he or she passes.

Chapter 3

What Is the Responsibility of the Doctor?

The "doctor" will refer to all providers, including nurse practitioners and physician assistants. It is important for the public to really know what a doctor does in his/her capacity as a provider. We are educated in a manner that will provide us with information that gives us the best opportunity to help the public in healthcare. It is the responsibility of each one of us to have up-to-date information so that we may advise and treat and care for another human being to the best of our abilities. We establish a relationship with the patient so that a level of trust can be developed and our advice will have a better chance of being followed in order to help the patient.

The very nature of bureaucratic intrusion into this doctor-patient relationship will undermine the trust that has developed over time, and the decision making process will no longer be in the control of, or guided by, the doctor-patient relationship. This relationship has constant checks and balances, since the doctor or provider is responsible for each and all actions and advice that he or she has given. The provider is constantly being watched by government agencies, insurance companies, pharmacies, and hospital quality control. Also, there is always a threat of a lawsuit if things go wrong. This cannot be said for a bureaucratic agency that will be immune to these checks and balances. This will result in decision making that will not be in the patient's best interest from a healthcare point of view. The bureaucratic agency will most likely utilize factors such as cost control to determine its decision-making.

Intrusion by bureaucrats hurts the patient more than the options provided by doctors and providers for patients in choosing the best mode of therapy. When the encounter between a provider and a patient is allowed, the choice for therapy is determined by a number of factors, of which costs is only one of the factors. The bureaucrat will inevitably not take the other factors such as age, overall health, family situation and support, and the patient's own personal decision making into account. The bureaucrats involved in this transformation of healthcare from the current Obama administration include Health and Human Services Secretary Kathleen Sebelius, Surgeon General Vice Admiral Regina Benjamin M.D., and Donald Berwick M.D.

Sec. Sebelius is a former governor of the state of Kansas and has a master's of public administration from the University of Kansas. It is doubtful that she is knowledgeable about the inner workings of healthcare regarding the relationship between the doctor and the patient and the importance of a strong and fair private sector in determining the best care for the citizens of our country. She is married to a judge and one can seriously question her healthcare experience other than from a political basis or agenda.

Surgeon General Dr. Regina Benjamin was trained in family practice. Family practitioners generally refer to specialists for care of their sicker patients. Many family practitioners are office-based and not involved with the majority of hospital care for patients. This means that family practitioners are important in the initial phase of healthcare by providing physicals, maintenance and preventative care, and taking care of the non-urgent medical issues. Specialists such as cardiologists, pulmonologists, or gastroenterologists, and others, do not have the time to take care of the primary care issues, physicals, and non-urgent medical issues, and attend to the patient with more severe and life-threatening problems. Therefore, it is fair to question whether Dr. Benjamin, as a Navy Officer with little exposure to the elderly in the military, has any significant experience regarding issues involving patients who have a serious illness, which include those in the hospital and those with multiple medical problems. These patients usually create the greatest cost to healthcare, especially in the last year of the patient's life, when a family practitioner's involvement with the patient is less. Dr. Benjamin also was on the AMA Board of Trustees before she turned forty and this usually leads to less direct patient care and more political involvement. It should be noted that family practice, internal medicine, and general surgery are projected to have an increase in payments in 2011 under Obamacare, where as it is unknown whether the other specialties will have any gains or in fact continue to have decreases in their reimbursement or payments. Therefore, will Dr. Benjamin really understand the issues involved and costs of end-of-life care without having firsthand experience?

Dr. Donald Berwick was appointed by the Obama administration during a recess, which means there was no Congressional approval, an obvious attempt by the Obama administration to avoid any checks and balances from Congress questioning a new appointment. His title is administrator of Centers for Medicare and Medicaid Services in the Department of Health and Human Services. Dr. Berwick is a firm believer in redistribution of wealth, and has publicly praised the current British healthcare system. In 2008, in front of a British audience, Dr. Berwick stated, "The decision is not whether or not we will ration care, the decision is whether we will ration with our eyes open. And right now, we are doing it blindly." Dr. Berwick was a pediatrician in Massachusetts, and in 1983 was a vice president of quality of care management. Dr. Berwick was in a nonprofit healthcare think tank back in 1989 in Massachusetts. This think tank was cofounded by Dr. Berwick and provided him with a $900,000 a year compensation package, including an executive retirement plan. As a pediatrician, it is fair to ask if he has ever taken care of a Medicare or elderly patient. It is safe to assume that there is a political agenda behind his appointment, which will result in a bureaucratic way of rationing in healthcare. That means that a politician's or bureaucrat's opinion, and the costs of the service, will be the determining factor in what type of treatment is available for the patient. As stated earlier, cost and political views are just a fraction of the things that are considered between the physician/provider and patient. Just like in all aspects of our lives as citizens in this country, we make decisions about purchasing houses or cars not just based on cost but on other factors such as location, education opportunities for the children, nearby family, job opportunities, and so on. It is always better to allow free choice by the individual rather than to have the choice imposed by a bureaucrat or even a physician acting as a bureaucrat.

Chapter 4

What Is Right with Obamacare?

There are many more things wrong with Obamacare than there are right with it. But, the healthcare discussion and legislation had to start somewhere. There is more coverage with an additional thirty-two million people insured by 2019. There is immediate coverage for children and gradual coverage for others. Children will now be able to be covered by their parents' insurance up until the age of twenty-six. There is now payment for healthcare screening in otherwise healthy individuals. This is to promote more preventative care in an effort to keep the nation healthier. Perhaps the best legislative item is no more pre-existing conditions can be utilized by the insurance companies in order to exclude coverage to a member. That is, insurance companies can no longer deny coverage for illnesses incurred prior to enrollment. The next best piece of legislative agenda in Obamacare is that insurance companies can no longer cap coverage; therefore, there will be no lifetime limits to cost of care. This will help people from becoming bankrupt from an illness. Also, prescription medications will become more affordable for Medicare enrollees. Those who use Medicare part D for prescriptions will have a $250 rebate in 2010. There will be a 50 percent discount on brand-name drugs in 2011. By 2020, there'll be a 75 percent discount on brand-name and generic medications. However, it is doubtful that most Medicare recipients who do not have a prescription plan and use Medicare part D will be able to afford any brand-name drugs since even with a 75 percent discount, many drugs will cost around $50 a month. Patients in the "donut hole" for use of their prescription medications most likely will have to use generic medications. These medications are less expensive and may only cost around $10 a month or less; however, they usually are of less quality compared to the brand-name medications and offer less choice to the patient.

Chapter 5

What Is Wrong with Obamacare?

There are many things wrong with Obamacare. They will be listed here and discussed separately.

1. Mandate to buy insurance
2. Increased taxes
3. Medicare cuts
4. Government involvement
5. Power of healthcare commissioner
6. No new incentives for providers
7. No meaningful malpractice reform
8. Overall costs to the economy
9. Medicaid cuts to hospitals
10. Interfering with physicians' self-referral
11. Education finance control added to the bill
12. More government involvement—unintended consequences

1. Insurance Mandate:

There has already been much discussion regarding a mandate for individuals to buy insurance who choose not to have insurance. Many individuals, especially youths, choose not to buy medical insurance because they choose to spend their money elsewhere. By 2016, individuals who have not acquired health insurance, either through their employer or on their own, will be subject to a fine, which may be $695 or as high as 2.5 percent of their income. Of course, anybody with common sense would realize that this is extremely unfair to force a segment of the population to buy a product or be fined if they choose not to buy the product. This leads to more hiring of government employees in the IRS to monitor American citizens, assuring they spend their money obtaining health insurance due to the government mandate.

In fact, there are now over twenty states that have sued the federal government based on the constitutionality of the insurance mandate provision in Obamacare. It is hopeful that this provision can be eliminated legally; then, the possibility of repealing the rest of Obamacare has a greater likelihood in 2013. All this country needs is another 16,500 government IRS workers intruding into our lives (16,500 is the number determined by the Joint Economic Committee and House Ways and Means Committee required to enforce the insurance mandate).

2. **Tax Increases:**

The bill increases taxes to businesses that make medical devices such as pacemakers and defibrillators with a new excise tax of 2.9 percent. There also is an increase in Medicare taxes for families with incomes over $250,000. As you know, this number is very dear to President Obama; he has stated many times that he considers families with over $250,000 in income as too rich and should be taxed more. Also, businesses will face up to $3000 in fines per employee for whom they do not provide health insurance coverage. This will hurt many businesses and will not achieve the goal of covering more Americans, as many businesses will opt to pay the fine or dismiss the employee altogether. This most likely will have the unintended consequence of causing businesses to hire fewer employees, which in turn will increase unemployment in our nation.

3.   **Medicare Cuts:**

There is a projected $500 billion in Medicare cuts, despite approximately seventy-two million more baby boomers added to Medicare over the next decade. There is no way that these cuts can be done without rationing care because of the increase number of Medicare recipients. Also making this issue more irrational is the fact that if the government gets more involved with regulating healthcare, there is certain to be a decrease in the number of providers, as many doctors will either leave the business or will retire earlier than anticipated. There will also be a 20 percent cut to Medicare A, which is the hospital portion for Medicare patients; this will also cause a decrease in services provided due to an increased number of patients.

There is no clear cost control mechanism or explanation as to where the cuts will be done. This means that, most likely, a bureaucrat will arbitrarily cut costs and, as stated previously, this will have negative effects on average American citizens by not allowing them to be in charge of their own health. Also, there will be unnecessary added costs when the government gets in the middle of healthcare decisions.

4. **Government Involvement:**

There are many hard working and dedicated people working in government. However, the nature of how government runs, without personal responsibility and accountability, enables bureaucrats (government officials) to be wasteful, counterproductive, and inefficient. The workers in government generally have their job well protected, even if their department has significant monetary losses. The bureaucrat can always ask for an increase in the budget next year to try to make up for any lost money since that money is coming from another source. That is, the taxpayers and American citizens. For example, everyone knows how well the US post office is doing with the billions of dollars it is losing each year; it is obviously poorly managed. It is illogical to think that, somehow, the bureaucrats in government will manage healthcare any better. As witnessed at the end of 2010 in New York City, after a significant snowstorm of close to two feet, many New Yorkers were held hostage by those that were supposed to clear the streets of snow. Many of the workers called in sick. This was three times the usual rate of sick calls for this department. This fact, together with a work slowdown, caused many New Yorkers to be trapped in streets of snow and ice, and created health problems for those needing ambulance and emergency care. Since there was to be a scheduled decrease/elimination of supervisors in the sanitation department in New York City in 2011 due to budget restraints, the unions (even though they deny it) appeared to punish the citizens of the city of New York with the sick calls and work slowdown. Does America really want to have the healthcare system placed in the hands of government workers who most likely will be unionized and control our health and well-being by their self-serving motives?

With Obamacare, bureaucrats will now be in a position of telling healthcare providers what to do. This practice is already done in the VA and in taking care of the criminals in our prison system. The VA does a very poor job taking care of its veterans who served our country and helped enable the rest of us Americans to have freedom and liberty. Any provider who has had experience with the VA knows that it is very hard for anyone who has a serious medical problem to get the proper medical attention in a timely manner. Not only is it hard to be referred to the right specialist, it is also hard to have the tests requested by the specialists performed quickly. For example, if a veteran has chest pain, which may indicate a serious heart condition, it may take months before seeing a cardiologist. It also takes months in many cases to get approval for the proper tests and procedures for that veteran. This causes obvious unnecessary pain and suffering and ends up becoming more costly for the healthcare system. A timely diagnosis in heart disease may prevent significant heart damage and many more costly complications in the long run. The more the government has control over both the decision-making process and the cost of healthcare, the more likely Americans will have less access to healthcare providers in a timely fashion for their health conditions. This will lead to more suffering and will lead to Americans dying earlier than necessary.

Because the Obamacare legislation is over two thousand pages and is not really understandable, more agencies will be added as time goes by, which will have even more of a negative impact. As if the establishment of over 150 new government agencies wasn't enough, two new bureaucratic agencies, since the bill was passed, include a Patient Centered Outcomes Research Institute and Independent Payment Advisory Board. These agencies will have the final word on what is good or appropriate care and have the power to reduce payments and ration care. A two-thirds vote by Congress will be necessary to repeal any decision made by the board. In other words, these agencies will be able to decide what is good for you and be able to manipulate reimbursement (payments) for procedures. This will influence or limit the choices you have as a patient. This can be done by withholding care, which will be disguised or deemed as too costly. These decisions will be made by a counsel/panel of experts. It seems to me that these experts will consist of yet more bureaucrats in these agencies. This can have a negative effect on life and death decisions. It is dangerous to place a bureaucrat in charge of life and death decisions at a time when Americans are most vulnerable. These decisions should be between a doctor and the patient and not legislated or decided by unqualified laypersons. It is necessary to have these decisions made by qualified personnel and the people involved—the physician and the patient. Therefore, in the best interest of all Americans, the relationship between a doctor and the patient should not be mandated by government personnel or agencies.

There is a degree of rationing that already exists in healthcare decisions, but market forces determine it, not government or politics. A decision to withhold care is appropriate at times. This decision should be based upon multiple factors. This includes the patient's wishes, family involvement, the physician or provider's recommendations, risks and benefits of additional care, and costs. The government should stay out of this aspect of healthcare since it is a private issue and not a political one.

5. **Power of Health Commissioner:**

The complexity and vagueness of the language involving the healthcare bill allow unprecedented power to a health commissioner appointed by the president. As stated earlier in Chapter 3, Dr. Berwick, as the administrative head of the Centers for Medicare and Medicaid Services, was a recess appointment by President Obama. Based on his public statements in the past, he is obviously in favor of a single payer system such as in Great Britain and believes in redistribution of wealth and government-controlled rationing. This belief that government can solve the problems of healthcare better than the private sector can, and that certain individuals in government know what is best for each individual American citizen concerning his or her own healthcare decisions, is a very dangerous belief. Again, our healthcare system and all Americans are best served when the system is not controlled by expanding government agencies, but by a private sector that is motivated by prior success to continue providing excellent medical care to the majority of Americans. Of course, cost constraints will limit the availability and quality of care in the future. This is why it is especially important to begin to fix the problems that are currently vexing our healthcare system in the US. The government is more a part of the problem rather than a part of the solution. This will be discussed in Chapters 7 and 8.

6. No New Incentives for Providers:

In the healthcare bill, there is no significant bureaucratic relief for primary healthcare providers. Because of the additional government agencies, it is obvious to anyone that has worked in healthcare that there will be more obstacles and more forms created. This will create more work, which will not be reimbursed, and will cause our primary healthcare providers to have less time to care for their patients. There will be longer wait times for patients since the primary care providers and doctors will have to do more paperwork and/or more documentation in the electronic medical record. Also, there is no education cost relief for physicians. Because of the high cost of medical education and the years of training, a physician will have an extraordinary amount of debt, which in many cases today is over $200,000. It is unlikely that many highly qualified students will want to become doctors in a financial setting where they will have a huge debt and only earn a forever-decreasing income after years of training and sacrifice. This will further decrease the number of physicians available and create longer wait times and more rationing of care.

7. No Meaningful Malpractice Reform:

There was no significant attempt to reform malpractice in the healthcare bill. The threat of malpractice is a real cost to healthcare. It causes providers to practice defensive medicine, which increases the costs for everyone. The malpractice attorneys were politically protected because of their strong allegiance to the Obama administration and to democrats in general. It is illogical to disregard malpractice reform when trying to curtail healthcare costs. The fact that malpractice reform was not addressed is obviously political and has nothing to do with an attempt to solve the problem of healthcare costs.

Malpractice tort reform can begin by capping pain and suffering settlements. This has been done successfully in several states, including Texas and California. Malpractice premiums for physicians can be decreased, and this would help avoid a short supply of certain subspecialties that have high malpractice insurance. For example, in Florida, there is a shortage of obstetricians because of the malpractice premiums. An obstetrician in Miami pays about $277,000 a year for malpractice insurance and one in Los Angeles pays about $63,000 a year. If malpractice insurance is high, then other costs of healthcare will be increased to offset a higher insurance premium paid by the physician for malpractice. Why are malpractice attorneys, who make up such a small percentage of the population, protected from making sacrifices and being part of the simplest solution for helping curtail healthcare costs? They will argue that malpractice is a small percentage of healthcare costs. That is simply not true. All doctors have had to practice defensive medicine because of the fear of litigation. Depending on the source, the fear of being sued and practicing defensive medicine can increase healthcare cost by $150 billion a year. Capping pain and suffering, like several states have done successfully without any increased harm to the public and patient, is a simple and practical way of decreasing healthcare costs. This will not increase the cost of healthcare in any way, but rather decrease it.

Also, tort reform should include removing the jury system by substituting a panel comprised of medical and legal experts, such as doctors and judges. These experts with their experience in the field are in a better position to determine guilt, and the panel would make more appropriate financial rewards in these malpractice cases as well. They are more likely to be unbiased by emotional aspects, as are many jury members. This would also decrease healthcare costs by eliminating the need for lengthy malpractice trials. Tort reform can decrease healthcare costs by both decreasing defensive medicine and decreasing the utilization of expensive technology, which only drive up the costs of healthcare.

8. **Overall Costs to the Economy:**

The healthcare bill is projected to add $940 billion to the deficit. Certain politicians have claimed that the bill will save money. It is known that Medicare and Medicaid, which are run by the government, are running deficits of their own. Anyone with common sense realizes that if you increase the number of people receiving healthcare, with agencies run by the government, the deficit will increase. So, what the government and those that passed the healthcare bill will not tell you directly is that there will need to be either a higher percentage of your income going to healthcare (meaning increased taxes) and/or there will be a rationing of healthcare with less services available and less people to deliver those services.

Also, with around 150 additional bureaucratic agencies, there will be increased bureaucratic layers between the provider and the patient, and this will naturally increase costs. Once these agencies are in place, it will be hard to remove them, and the costs will continue to go up to support these agencies. This will help the government workers in these agencies keep their jobs, but will hurt America's healthcare system, as less money will be available to care for the population.

9. Medicaid Cuts to Hospitals:

In 2014, there will be $4 billion dollars less paid to hospitals in Medicaid payments. As of now, the hospitals lose money with Medicaid payments, which they received from both the federal and state governments. The costs incurred by a hospital for providing service to a Medicaid patient are more than the money it receives. So giving less money to the hospitals will only cause less revenue to the hospitals, and many more hospitals will be financially strapped and have to close. This will also cause employees to be without jobs, which does not help the current unemployment rate. Since 2008, when unemployment began increasing significantly, the number of Medicaid recipients in our country has also increased significantly, to almost fifty million Americans. Medicaid payment rates to hospitals and doctors and other providers have been cut or frozen in most states. The Medicaid payment rates are so low that it is getting harder to find a doctor who will accept Medicaid coverage. Therefore, doctors will be donating their services for free at the hospital for these patients, as they do for many self-pay patients. The hospitals are less in a position to offer free or reduced care. This will cause a crisis at some point in time and it is hard to imagine that the system can continue if it keeps going in this direction of decreasing payments and decreasing available providers.

10. **Interfering with Physician's Self-referral:**

Hospitals that are owned by physicians will be affected in 2011. No new ones can be built. This is an attempt to decrease the private sector of healthcare and to gradually have publicly/government-controlled healthcare. A better strategy would be to let other hospitals compete with these physician-owned hospitals and let the market forces, through competition, determine the outcome, rather than the government limiting choices for the individual. By making it more difficult for the private sector to survive through selective legislation harming the private industry, the goal will be to have most providers working for hospitals. This will decrease competition and cause more centralization of the services, and it will be easier for the government to eventually obtain control.

Also, there is a significant decrease in Medicare payments to physicians who are paid through Medicare part B for the same service as with Medicare part A. Medicare part B is for services rendered by a physician/provider. Medicare part A is for services provided by a hospital. For example, a cardiologist who has an ultrasound or echocardiogram in his office and performs the study on a patient in his office will be reimbursed or paid about 20 to 30 percent less than if it was done in the hospital. This is because Medicare part A has higher pay rates for the same procedure in many cases. Not only is this more costly, but it does not allow the patient to choose where he or she wants to go to have a procedure done.

This provision of the healthcare bill will not decrease costs, but rather increase costs when healthcare is more centralized with a massive bureaucracy controlling a significant portion of the American economy. Healthcare costs can be kept lower only through the private sector and competition. When the government competes, it does not close when it fails. The government simply takes more money from citizens, prints more money, or borrows more money. This philosophy does not bode well for a healthy American future, as it only increases the chances for failure.

11. Education Finance Control Added to the Bill:

When Congress was discussing what needed to be included in the healthcare bill, somehow financing education in our country was considered a part of healthcare. This provision to the bill is for the government to have control of student loans. The government essentially has cut out the banks and become the main lender. As you know, the government does a great job being in control of lending. After all, they have done such an outstanding job being the main lenders for housing mortgages with Fannie Mae and Freddie Mac, who we know are mainly responsible for the current housing crisis in our country.

12. More Government Involvement—Unintended Consequences:

It cannot be emphasized enough how more government involvement will create more costs through its mismanagement and waste. This will have unintended consequences that have not yet been foreseen. For example, when a patient feels that his or her healthcare is a right and that he/she is entitled to it without any financial or personal responsibilities, he/she will abuse that privilege and go to the doctor often for minor ailments. This will cause additional waiting time for more patients who really need the care to increase. This will create a form of rationing on a first-come, first-serve basis and will decrease the quality of care that a provider can deliver for the patient. This is already occurring with the Medicaid population. Many feel that they shouldn't have to pay even a $3 copayment to see a doctor when they want to. Since the Medicaid population is increasing significantly, this will further cause delays in rendering proper and appropriate care. Since Medicaid operates mostly at a financial loss, the unintended consequences in the long run are that less Americans will have appropriate and timely access to healthcare. This is because there will be less doctors willing to provide service to Medicaid patients because of the financial losses incurred. For those that do provide service to Medicaid patients, it will be a sacrifice for all the other patients who now, because of the increased demand of the number of patients with fewer providers, will have longer waiting times and rationing, which will result in a decrease to their quality of care.

Other unintended consequences that have a negative impact on the private sector are:

a) Employers will be required to disclose the value of health benefits on W-2 forms of employees beginning in 2011. This increases costs and leads to unnecessary paperwork.

b) Companies will be required in 2012 to issue 1099 forms to the IRS and to any vendor of services greater than $600. This will increase the paperwork and potential fines, and also increase government oversight. (At this time, this provision is under consideration for repeal).

c) For companies with more than fifty employees, beginning in 2014, there will be a fine of $2000 per employee not covered by the employer. Companies may not hire more once they get to fifty employees, so as not to face these fines. This is a disincentive for a successful growing business. Many companies, like McDonalds, may instead choose to pay a fine, which defeats the purpose of trying to get more people health insurance.

d) There will be an excise tax on high-cost employer health plans. This will discourage further competition and the emergence of better insurance plans for those who can afford it. This is an obvious attempt to redistribute the wealth and is totally un-American. It is a disguised attempt to creep more and more toward a single payer system.

Other unintended or "intended" consequences are the exceptions or waivers for companies that have been favorable to President Obama. Exceptions to some of the provisions have been made for companies such as those with high union membership who have been very supportive of President Obama. The waiver should be given to President Obama from continuing his presidency past 2012.

Chapter 6

What Is the Responsibility of Government?

The intentions of the founding fathers were a limited government and that the government follows the will of its people, who are the citizens of this great nation. Were the November elections in 2010 a referendum on Obamacare? The majority of Americans rejected the concept that government can make choices for us in healthcare and rejected the concept that government involvement in healthcare will result in the system becoming more affordable and more available to it citizens.

Even though ideologically, it is a noble concept to insure all Americans, it needs to be done in a way that the majority of Americans will not suffer in the long run. The administration and Congress in 2010 did not understand the reality that helping a small percentage of Americans initially at the expense of the majority of Americans will eventually lead to all Americans having less care available. This is because of an unintended increase in rationing due to a decrease in the number of providers and an increase in regulations resulting from increased bureaucracy.

The healthcare debate should have focused more on the rising costs of healthcare and how Congress can change the tax laws and regulations so that a greater percentage of Americans can obtain insurance. In this way, the future of healthcare in this country has a better chance of remaining solvent and continuing to provide excellent care.

Chapter 7

What Is the Track Record of Government's Involvement in Healthcare?

There are numerous examples of how poorly the government is doing with its current involvement with healthcare. The Veterans Administration is run by the government and is a good example of what happens to the costs and the quality of care when the government is in charge. The VA is good for healthy veterans who just need physicals, blood work, and generic medications. They get this care for free and it is of great service to those that served in the military to defend our liberty and freedom. Unfortunately, most of the veterans are elderly and have significant medical problems and illnesses, and require a lot more testing and more appropriate brand-name medications for their conditions. Many don't receive timely and appropriate care. As a cardiologist, I am requested to consult on patients referred from the VA. Because of the many forms necessary to be approved by a bureaucrat and the resulting delay in obtaining appropriate tests or procedures to help an ailing veteran, he/she inevitably receives substandard care. This is done in an effort to save money, but this strategy backfires, such as when heart conditions are not dealt with in a preventative manner, the healthcare costs increase significantly.

Also, the money the government (VA) perceives it is saving by making it more difficult for the veteran to obtain proper and timely care is being wasted on programs and expenditures that did not create any benefit for the veteran.

For example, I am aware of a VA clinic built in Las Vegas based on suggestions by bureaucrats and physicians that attended the planning meetings. If a particular physician was too busy to attend a meeting regarding the building and space available for his or her department, then that department received fewer funds. It was not based on what was needed for the veterans and which medical departments may need to be bigger because of the demand and need for that service. Rather, it was based on who was at the planning meetings and who had the better connections. Also, if the planning team changed its mind, the construction and work would have been redone at a much higher expense. This way of doing business is absurd. This does not help the bottom line, which is the healthcare of the veterans, which is what the money was intended for in the first place. There have also been examples of huge expenditures for women's services for these VA clinics (namely for the wives of serviceman). This was done even though many women choose to go to their own private doctor rather than use the VA.

Another example of waste by the VA is a known practice by bureaucratic administrators. They ask for more money each year, even if it is not needed, so that their allotment of the monies given does not decrease. They purposely go over budget and spend more money so that they can ask for more money in the following year's budget. At times, bureaucrats' offices are refurnished unnecessarily in an effort to justify asking for more money. Many times, supplies that had not been used and are still functional will be replaced in another effort to justify the need to obtain a higher budget.

Because of the inability of the government to monitor fraud and waste, there are many more examples of why the government should not control healthcare. It is estimated that $20 billion annually is wasted by Medicare providers because of inaccurate billing practices and payments for non-covered services, phantom procedures, and phantom patient bills.

Also, since Medicare drug plan D went into effect, more fraud has been perpetrated.

In California, it is estimated that there is approximately $1 billion of Medicaid fraud annually. New York State is close to $1 billion in extra costs from fraud and abuse as well. With respect to Medicaid nursing home benefits, higher income seniors hide assets in order to qualify for services. Nationally, it is estimated that this creates $10 billion in extra costs to the taxpayer per year.

These are just some of the examples of waste and mismanagement. This can never help to decrease the costs of healthcare and can only add to the costs, which further cause a decrease in the quality and delivery of care.

Chapter 8

Is Increasing the Bureaucracy the Answer?

Since the presidential election in 2008, the government has grown bigger at a faster rate than ever before in our history. There was an economic downturn in 2008 with increasing unemployment rates. Yet, the only sector that has had any significant increase in jobs in 2009 and 2010 were government jobs. The government and the bureaucracy do not create wealth in our country, but rather the private sector and free enterprise system do. There is a need for Americans to demand of their legislative leaders to downsize the federal government now, before it is too late to do so in a cost effective and efficient manner and before there are dire consequences leading to lack of basic services—especially those services such as defending our nation, establishing justice, insuring domestic tranquility, and securing the blessing of liberty, which were enumerated initially by our founding fathers in our constitution.

There are many more examples of government waste and fraud not involving healthcare. In an effort to eliminate fraud, the government requires more regulation and oversight, which then requires more money, which is run by bureaucrats, which further complicates the costs. The Defense Department commonly loses track of its assets, has excess inventory, underestimates costs of projects, and overpays contractors. With respect to farm subsidies, it is estimated that up to $500 million a year of inappropriate subsidies are handed out. Also, Social Security estimates to have over $1 billion dollars of fraud yearly, such as benefits that go to individuals who are already dead. FEMA, which stands for Federal Emergency Management Agency, loses millions yearly to fraud and poor management. In some cases, these were indiscriminate handouts, like credit cards handed out to victims from Hurricane Katrina who then used them to go to strip clubs at the government's expense, which is the taxpayers' expense.

Also, the bureaucracy and government expansion duplicates many programs. A Senate committee on government affairs discovered that there are twenty-seven programs for teen pregnancy, nineteen programs for the prevention of substance abuse, and 342 programs for economic development. This increase in the number of programs and their budget allocations causes more self-serving and wasteful decisions in order for government workers to keep their jobs, which in turn creates more wasteful spending.

Increasing the bureaucracy is a very costly proposition for any government, let alone one that should be run by limited government and for the people. The average worker in the government earns $74,000 a year, while in the private sector, the average worker earns $50,000 a year. This makes the average government worker more dependent on the government and distrustful of free enterprise or the private sector. When more agencies are created because of a perceived need at the time, the agency then becomes more determined to keep its own survival rather than serve the people it was meant to serve in the first place. This leads to more centralized control and less liberty for any individual.

Bureaucracies do not have a good track record of being able to estimate the cost of government programs. For instance, Medicare part A, which began in 1965, had a projected cost of $9 billion in 1990. The actual cost was $67 billion, over seven times more than what was predicted. A Medicaid special hospital subsidy, which was added in 1987, had a projected cost of $100 million annually. However, by 1992, the cost was $11 billion annually, over one hundred times more than predicted. Also, government officials or bureaucrats tend to make decisions based on costs and not medical necessity. In early December 2010, there were Medicaid cuts in Arizona. Organ transplants were eliminated from coverage. The major factor in making these cuts was money/budget related and the decision was not made based on medical need. This action caused denial to individuals who may have been in life or death situations. As stated previously, it is dangerous to leave these types of decisions to bureaucrats. It is always better to leave these decisions between the doctor and the patient. It seems obvious that if we decreased the size of government and saved the expenditure of many unnecessary, duplicate, or wasteful agencies there would be more money available to be used for individuals who were in life and death situations and in need of a possible heart, liver, or bone marrow transplant.

Section II

What Are the Solutions?

In dealing with the solutions for healthcare, Congress, in 2010, conveniently did not even include the two most obvious solutions, which would not cost the taxpayer a dime—selling insurance across state lines and tort reform. Call me skeptical, but I believe it has something to do with both the lobbying and political interests of the insurance companies, the American Bar Association and Democrats.

Chapter 9

Insurance Across State Lines

The healthcare of the citizens of our country is not a state issue, but a national one. The choice of an insurance plan should be up to the individual and not up to the state or national government. This is best achieved by allowing health insurances to compete across state lines. This will allow for healthy competition and lower cost. No longer will there be a monopoly with few insurance companies having leverage within an individual state. There will no longer be deals between an individual state and insurer. These deals or arrangements inevitably help some insurance companies and bureaucrats, but not the individuals in the state needing healthcare. For example, Alabama has very few major insurance agents and is not a very healthy state. According to the United Health Foundation survey in 2009, Alabama ranked forty-fifth of the healthiest states to live in the US. Forty-fifth out of fifty states is not very impressive and shows the need for better options by allowing insurance across state lines.

One should remember that life insurance and car insurance is purchased across state lines, and this allows for competitive rates and for individual choices. Since consumers of healthcare already are allowed to obtain care in other states besides the one they live in, Congress will only need to remove the states from having primary regulatory authority over health insurance. Consumers will then be able to buy less-expensive policies in other states. In allowing health insurers to compete across state lines, the insurers will also have to adapt to each states' consumer protection laws, since they are different from state to state.

If insurance companies are allowed to compete across state lines, it will be easier to have portability of health insurance. This means that an individual can change jobs in any part of our country and maintain his or her insurance. Also, this allows for more flexibility for the employer. As of now, there are about 159 million Americans who obtain insurance and are covered through their employer. The employers pick one insurance company to provide coverage for their employees. If Obamacare is not repealed, over time, the employer will pick the least expensive plan. The plan most likely selected will be one of the government plans because private healthcare insurers would not be able to compete with the government plans. This is because the government does not follow the same market principals as the private sector. They are a monopoly and cannot fail, even if they lose money. Over time, these government plans only become more costly and riddled with increasing debt. This is precisely what has already happened with the VA and with Medicare and Medicaid.

The employee does not have any options for choosing his/her healthcare insurer. By being able to purchase health insurance across state lines and by having portability, there will be more choices for the employee to have the healthcare plan most affordable and most appropriate for himself/herself and his/her family. The employer can be responsible for a portion of the employee's healthcare premium as it is currently set up. But if the employee has a plan that is different than the employer's, the employee can choose to use the employer's plan or use the money put aside by the employer for healthcare benefits to help pay for the premiums of the healthcare plan of his/her own choosing. This way, the employee is in control of the healthcare plan that he or she wishes to keep for himself/herself and his/her family.

Also, there should be tax benefits for both the employer and employee purchasing their own plan and not using a government subsidized plan. A portion of the insurance premiums should be tax deductible. By enabling the employer and employee to have tax benefits, more Americans will have private insurance, which will decrease the need for more Americans being on government subsidized insurance. The employers would benefit by having lower overall health insurance outlays, which will enable them to keep more employees employed. This will improve unemployment in our country. As of now, there are hundreds of companies that have received waivers from mandating them to cover their employees' health benefits because they know they cannot afford it under Obamacare. There are also many companies that will opt to pay the fine instead of covering their employees' health insurance, simply because they know they cannot afford it. If many of these companies are forced to obtain coverage for their employees under Obamacare, there will be less hiring and possibly more firing, which will further cause a rise in unemployment and not help address the problem of increasing the number of Americans covered with health insurance.

There was a report by the CBO in 2005 that if all individuals picked their health insurance from states with the lowest benefit mandates, it would only reduce the cost of their health insurance by about 5 percent on the average. Maybe for the CBO, 5 percent less is not a lot, but for the average citizens it is a step in the right direction.

Chapter 10

Tort Reform

I discussed earlier in the book why tort reform was not discussed to any significant degree in Obamacare. Anyone that has any knowledge of healthcare understands the impact that malpractice has on the cost of healthcare. There have been estimates that malpractice adds up to an extra $150 billion a year to the cost of healthcare because of the practice of defensive medicine and because of the number of frivolous lawsuits.

Malpractice has both direct and indirect costs. The direct costs involve the malpractice insurance premiums the doctors have to pay and the costs of the income lost when a doctor has to prepare for a lawsuit and cannot work and earn income. The indirect costs involve the concept of defensive medicine. Defensive medicine is practiced every day by physicians and providers because of the threat of litigation and, at times, an unrealistic expectation by the public for a particular health problem. For example, a patient may have a headache and see his regular physician who is very familiar with his symptoms. After the examination, the physician determines that it is not a life-threatening headache and orders some medication for the patient and a follow up visit. The patient then decides to go to the emergency room because he does not feel immediately better. The emergency room physician, who is not familiar with this patient, who has these complaints frequently, then decides to obtain a battery of tests, including lab work and a CAT scan of the head. The chances that the tests would be abnormal or cost effective are very low, probably under 1 percent. Unfortunately, many physicians unfamiliar with a patient who has recurrent symptoms will order a battery of tests because they do not want to take any chances that they might miss a diagnosis, even if the odds are less than 1 percent.

The AMA has estimated that 10 percent of the total US cost of healthcare is attributable to malpractice and close to 8 percent of that 10 percent is due to the practice of defensive medicine.

In other countries that have universal healthcare or socialized medicine, there is not the abundance of malpractice lawyers as there is in this country. In fact, there are very few malpractice lawyers, and one does not see in these countries the numerous commercials that enhance a lawyer's reputation for being ambulance chasers. Also, in many of these countries, such as England and Australia, when there is a malpractice case, the loser pays all the costs of litigation. This decreases the amount of frivolous lawsuits. It is estimated that over 80 percent of the lawsuits in our country are frivolous.

There are three main components to any meaningful tort reform.

a) **Capping Pain and Suffering**

This has been utilized successfully in several states such as Texas and California. In California for example, an obstetrician in LA when compared to Miami Florida, pays about $200,000 less a year for malpractice insurance. Not only does this increase healthcare costs—by offsetting the high malpractice premiums with fees for other services so that the obstetrician in Miami can practice medicine—but, there is a decrease in public safety. Obstetricians are in short supply in states such as Florida because of these high malpractice premiums and this places many Americans and their unborn children at an increased and unnecessary risk. In Texas, after passing medical liability reform in 2003, emphasizing a cap for pain and suffering, there was a 58 percent increase in the number of doctors who came to Texas over a five-year period. There was also a 7.2 percent increase in obstetrics/gynecology physicians over a five-year period. And, there was a 25 percent drop in the medical liability rates. Congress needs to follow the example of states that have malpractice caps for pain and suffering because it is more fair and more effective in containing costs without decreasing the quality of care.

b) Using Jury Panels

North Carolina had the pleasure of having John Edwards practice malpractice law. He would often take cases that had bad outcomes so that he could evoke the most sympathy and be granted the highest rewards. Many of these cases were maternity suits where babies were born with abnormalities. These abnormalities may have nothing to do with the delivery of care provided by the doctor or the hospital. By simply displaying the baby's handicap, the jury, usually on an emotional basis, would award a huge settlement under the pain and suffering provision.

As stated earlier in this book, the jury system for malpractice should be substituted with a panel comprised of three to five medical and legal experts such as doctors and judges. These experts are in a better position to determine guilt or innocence and they are better qualified to make more appropriate financial rewards in malpractice cases since they are unbiased with less emotional ties. They also will be less likely fooled by a lawyer's attempt at evoking sympathy in order to obtain a higher financial reward. Also, this panel can review the case before it goes to trial so that cases that do have legitimate malpractice can be settled and the extra costs involved in a trial will be spared. This panel can also determine which lawsuits are frivolous and recommend to the judge to dismiss the case.

c) Adopting the Loser Pays System

If lawyers who took malpractice cases on contingency had to also pay the defendant's fees if these defendants were dropped from the lawsuit or found innocent, there would be a significant decrease in frivolous lawsuits. In many lawsuits, every doctor involved in the case is named as a defendant and then deposed, in the hopes of getting some information that can be used against that doctor. The purpose of naming doctors that were only marginally involved in the case is to get as much free information as possible. The lawyer is going to name as many doctors who have good malpractice insurance (deep pockets) as possible to increase his/her chances of getting damaging information that can lead to higher financial rewards. If these lawyers had to pay the legal fees for the doctors who were later dropped before the trial, or pay for the doctors/defendants that were determined to be innocent, then I am sure that the malpractice lawyers would be more selective in whom they choose to sue for malpractice. This is because the odds won't be stacked in their favor and they will actually have something to lose when they are wrong.

The goal of medical malpractice should be to determine whether malpractice has actually occurred and what the appropriate financial reward or compensation for the damages or injury should be.

If these three items were implemented with tort reform, there would be lower costs to both the doctor/provider and also to the patient, since the overall cost of healthcare will then be decreased. This will not have a negative impact on the quality of care. The only negative impact will be less malpractice attorneys who are multimillionaires.

Chapter 11

No Exclusions for Preexisting Conditions:

It is important that an individual should not be excluded from obtaining health insurance because of pre-existing conditions. Federal law already prohibits employers from discriminating against employees and their dependent family members based on any health factors they may have, including prior medical conditions. Insurance companies should not be able to cherry pick who they cover and who they do not cover. Insurance companies will always try to pick healthier patients because they want to collect the premiums and keep health costs at a minimum, so that they can make higher profits. If we are going to maintain the quality of healthcare at an affordable rate, then certain sacrifices will need to be made by all those involved in healthcare, including the insurance companies, the pharmaceutical companies, the health supply companies, the providers, the hospitals, and the lawyers.

A recent study by the Department of Health and Human Services demonstrated that as many as 129 million

Americans under the age of sixty-five had some type of pre-existing health condition. Also, there is an aging population, which will increase this number of Americans with pre-existing conditions. Since this applies to almost one in two Americans, it would be unfair to exclude this high a percentage of Americans from obtaining healthcare simply because they have pre-existing conditions.

When insurance companies have to take patients with pre-existing conditions, this will allow individuals to obtain the insurance of their choice, depending on which insurance in the country best suits their needs for their particular health condition. Anyone who obtains life insurance knows that if they are older or have poor health or risky behavior, life insurance premiums will be more costly for a certain amount of life insurance coverage. The same should be true with healthcare. Americans should be allowed to smoke if they wish, but should realize that if they do, they incur a higher risk of health problems and, therefore, their insurance premiums will be higher. There will need to be a national health insurance panel to determine the degree of risk with each lifestyle habit and with each pre-existing condition. The risk would be assigned in the same manner as actuaries (evaluating the likelihood of future events) do with life insurance. There would be a ceiling as to how high the premiums could be; but, an individual with more pre-existing conditions and/or unhealthy and proven more costly health habits would expect to pay more for his or her health insurance policy.

Insurance companies should obtain some tax benefits for insuring more Americans who are at higher risk. Just like individual Americans should obtain some tax relief for paying for their premiums, the insurance companies should receive a tax benefits for covering higher risk patients and including them with less costly lower risk patients. This would hopefully alleviate the need for government involvement in creating insurance programs specifically for higher risk patients. As stated earlier, when the government gets more involved with controlling healthcare, the long-term costs become more than anticipated, and choices for the individual become more limited.

In September 2010, insurers were not able to exclude children with pre-existing conditions. This same rule applies for adults beginning January 1, 2014. Therefore, there is a window of opportunity to repeal Obamacare and still include provisions such as no exclusions for pre-existing conditions and many of the other solutions mentioned in this chapter by 2014. That is why it will be important to have a president who will begin his/her presidency in 2013 with a pledge of repealing Obamacare and substituting it with the provisions that were good in Obamacare and include many new provisions that are market driven with private-sector involvement rather than government control.

With respect to all children up to the age of twenty-six being included on their parents' plan, I have a few comments to make. While I find it somewhat ironic that the government would consider individuals between the ages of eighteen and twenty-six "children," for the sake of healthcare coverage, I do feel that parents should be able to cover children that are pursuing an education up until their twenty-sixth birthday so that the value of getting an education is encouraged and rewarded. Including all children, especially those that are working and those that may be married, seems a bit much. Do we need a nanny state for adults under age twenty-six?

Chapter 12

Cap for Catastrophic Care

Catastrophic cap or limit is the maximum amount that an individual will have to pay out of pocket per fiscal year (generally from October 1 to September 30) to the health insurance company. Right now, most insurance companies will only cover an individual up to a certain amount of healthcare coverage. If an individual surpasses that amount, the responsibility of payment goes to that individual. This is why many individuals have become bankrupt after a serious illness. Just like with pre-existing conditions, it is inherently unfair that individuals can become bankrupt from an illness. The overall costs should be absorbed mainly by the insurance companies. However, there will need to be an upper cap, such as $1 million in a year per policy, so that the insurance company is not completely overexposed to exorbitant fees.

For individuals who are not on Medicare or Medicaid, or on government assistance programs, the limit in a fiscal year may be up to $20,000; or in individuals with assets over $100,000, the limit can increase by 10 percent of their assets over $100,000 until the bill is paid. Therefore, the costs will be distributed among the individual and the health insurance company. As of now, when an individual cannot pay his or her health bill, the costs are being redistributed by increasing premiums to others covered by private health insurance companies. This way of income redistribution does not help the individual who now faces bankruptcy. This also creates unintended consequences after individuals become bankrupt by having them more dependent on the government's tab and, thus, creating less productivity in society as a whole.

Chapter 13

Entry Age for Medicare

When Medicare began in 1965, the life expectancy for men was under sixty-seven and for women it was under seventy-four; the average was under seventy-one years of age. Today, life expectancy is close to seventy-five for men and eighty for women. Reuters, in August 2009, reported that the average life expectancy at that time was 77.9 for all people in the United States. Therefore, over the last forty-five years, the life expectancy has increased over seven years.

In order to keep Medicare solvent, steps will need to be done now to help insure its future. Those steps include increasing the Medicare entry age at least five more years so that it is at age seventy for those individuals who are currently under forty-five years of age or those born after 1968 (if a bill passes in 2013). For those individuals between forty-five and fifty-five years of age, there will be a gradual increase of one year for every two years of age. Assuming that the Medicare entry age will be changed in 2013, it will be age sixty-six for those born after 1958, sixty-seven for those born after 1960, sixty-eight for those born after 1962, sixty-nine for those born after 1964, and seventy for all Americans born after December 31, 1966.

It is only logical to increase the Medicare entry age since the population is living longer and can work longer and be more productive. In 1965, when the average life expectancy was close to age seventy-one, individuals usually retired at age sixty-five. Now that the average life expectancy is close to age seventy-eight, this means that people are healthier today and can work longer. Therefore, it makes sense for a healthier and more productive nation to encourage its citizens to remain active by continuing to work up until the age of seventy. This will accomplish two major things. One, it will produce more revenue for the nation because its citizens will remain longer in the work force and remain productive. Two, as a physician, it is apparent to me that when people work longer, they remain healthier for a longer period of time. This will also help decrease health costs by having fewer individuals in retirement having more health problems than their counterparts who are working.

Of course, it is difficult for politicians to do the right thing and make the necessary changes to keep programs viable in the future. They have been afraid to tackle Medicare and other entitlements in a mature, responsible, and intelligent manner because they are, in general, more fearful of losing votes than in doing the right thing for Americans. That is why it is extremely important in 2012 to vote for candidates that have pledged that they are willing to vote and pass the necessary laws to keep America's favorite programs viable and solvent in the future.

Chapter 14

Medicare Coverage with Advancing Age

As individuals get older, their healthcare costs increases. It is usually in the last year of one's life when the majority of healthcare costs ensue. The costs covered by Medicare are about five times higher in the last year of life than they are in the previous years. This is due to several reasons.

a) <u>Unrealistic expectations.</u> There is a need to educate the patient and family about realistic expectations. Too often, the patient and family members expect everything to be done in order to remain alive. Sometimes when a patient is at the end of life, comfort care is actually more merciful and less painful. Procedures that are done in order to prolong a life are not only expensive, but in many cases painful and harmful to the patient. If the patient and family members knew what the alternatives were when faced with end-of-life decisions, there would be more informed decisions made when a crisis arises. Since it is difficult to have a discussion with the patient and family members during a serious illness toward the end of one's life, this discussion should take place earlier, when the patient is healthier and in his or her private doctor's office. A specialist who is called upon to help this patient in the hospital usually does not know the patient or the family well and it is difficult for him/her to give appropriate advice as to how aggressive or nonaggressive one should be with conditions that may be life threatening. A discussion in the office can take place between a doctor and the patient once the patient is of Medicare age or has a pre-existing condition that may result in a life-threatening situation in the near future. This discussion should be reimbursed appropriately by Medicare or the insurance company since these discussions lead to more informed decisions by the patients and, in many cases, would decrease the costs significantly. These discussions already occur between the doctor and the patient in many cases. By reimbursing the discussion between a doctor and a patient, it is likely that it will be done more often because of the additional financial incentive. Hence it will result in more cost-effectiveness in the long run. This type of discussion should not be mistaken for the misperception of it being a "death panel discussion." I believe that death panels pertain to situations where bureaucrats and not doctors and/or patients are making end of life decisions. These bureaucrats will base their decisions regarding end-of-life options on ideology and financial considerations and not on the overall medical conditions and the particular situation involved with this individual.

b) <u>Expensive costs of highly technical services and intensive care services in a hospital.</u> Naturally, if the option of "living at all costs" is preferred over the quality of one's life at the end of life, the amount of resources to keep a person alive will be costly. Being in the intensive care unit for a serious illness is very costly because of the added expenses involved in the use of equipment such as respirators and all the diagnostic testing necessary to make a diagnosis and treatment. If the family and patient understood better all the options available in providing more comfort at the end of one's life rather than more testing and potential pain and suffering, they might choose treatment geared at comfort, which in many cases will be more humane and also less costly.

Because of the additional costs in healthcare that occurs with advancing age, I propose that the Medicare, which is now 80 percent, begin to decrease down to 70 percent beginning at the age of eighty-five. That is, at age eighty-five, Medicare coverage would be at 78 percent, and at age ninety, it would be down to 70 percent. Usually, the remaining 20 percent is either picked up by Medicaid (the government) or by a private insurer. The patient can pay higher premiums to get the extra 10 percent coverage, or if necessary, will need to pay out of pocket. This will discourage family members from asking for everything being done when they have more of a financial stake in the decision. Many times, a decision to do expensive procedures on very elderly patients make the family members feel like they are doing something, and may alleviate some guilt, but it does not actually prolong a loved one's (patient's) life or improve a patient's quality of care.

Chapter 15

Means Testing for Medicare Beneficiaries

Many people over the age of sixty-five, or eventually seventy if the entry age for Medicare is increased in 2013, have the ability to pay higher premiums for the same level of service if they are wealthy. That is, there should be a means test for the amount of coverage Medicare will provide for the elderly. The easiest way to do that is to determine the percentage that Medicare will cover. As stated earlier, Medicare covers 80 percent of the healthcare expenses for part A and part B. This pertains to the hospital and physician/provider expenses.

I propose that individual Medicare beneficiaries who have assets over $250,000 and less than $500,000, have 80 percent coverage at less than $250,000 and 75 percent coverage between $250,000 and $500,000. There would be a percentage point drop for each $50,000 of individual assets a person has over $250,000, up to $500,000. For example, an individual with $300,000 in assets would have only 79 percent coverage from Medicare for his part A and part B.

An individual with $400,000 in assets would have 77 percent coverage. I start at $250,000 because that is Obama's magic number, the limit where he thinks people have too much ($250,000 a year).

Individuals with over $500,000 of assets and less than $1 million of assets would have 75 percent coverage decreasing to 65 percent at $1 million. For example, an individual with $750,000 of assets would have 70 percent Medicare coverage.

Individuals with over a million dollars of assets would decrease from 65 percent coverage down to 50 percent coverage at $5 million of assets. Over $5 million of assets, the coverage remains at 50 percent. It could always be lowered with increasing assets in the future.

Therefore, individuals with over $250,000 of assets can help offset some of the costs of Medicare by paying more into healthcare. They can pick up private health insurance, which will cover the additional 10 to 30 percent not covered by Medicare.

To some, this may seem like redistribution of wealth. However, I believe it is important for those people in our country who have the ability to pay for more insurance on their own to do so. In this way, the poor can have better coverage since there will be a cost savings with less Medicare revenue being paid out to many who can afford it. This is especially important because of the increase in the aging population, with approximately seventy-two million baby boomers over the age of the sixty-five by 2019.

Chapter 16

Health Savings Accounts

Health savings accounts are tax-free medical savings accounts. These accounts are owned by the individual and the contribution to these health savings accounts (HSAs) is done on a pretax basis. Therefore, they are not subject to federal taxes when one deposits them. These health savings accounts are used in conjunction with a high-deductible health insurance plan. The funds can be withdrawn for medical expenses and they can be invested and growing indefinitely. For some HSAs, if the funds are not used in a calendar year, they will roll over and can be used at any time in the future. They also have a maximum out-of-pocket limit for both individual and family coverage.

Obamacare has had a negative effect on these health savings accounts. The funds can no longer be used to buy over-the-counter medications. This is totally absurd since it is cheaper, in many cases, for people not to use prescribed medications and use over-the-counter, less expensive medications. Also, the health saving accounts for Medicare is being affected by increasing its cost significantly and making it less attractive to purchase. I believe the reason for this is to try to take the control of making healthcare decisions away from the individual and place them in the hands of government.

I propose that health savings accounts and Medicare savings accounts should be liberalized and have even more tax benefits. If an individual uses a health savings account earlier in life, he or she will have more control over his/her healthcare decisions and costs. This can only benefit the overall costs of healthcare by having individuals more informed and by having to be more cost conscious since it is their own savings they are dipping into when using the healthcare system.

When individuals use a health savings account during their life, it is more likely they will use Medicare savings accounts when they are of age. This will help keep Medicare costs down; and the population will be more in control of their health and more cost conscious, and consequently will most likely be healthier.

Chapter 17

Allow Medicare Advantage

In 1997, legislation was passed to allow Medicare beneficiaries the option of receiving their Medicare benefits with private health insurance plans. They would receive their benefits through these Medicare advantage plans instead of through Medicare parts A and B. As of March 2010, over eleven million people were enrolled in Medicare advantage plans. This represents about 25 percent of Medicare beneficiaries.

Obamacare does away with many of the government subsidies for Medicare advantage plans, thereby essentially causing the program to be eliminated over time. Cigna and other insurance companies have already indicated they will not continue their Medicare advantage plans. Again, this was another example of government trying to destroy the private sector and private insurance and have more control over individuals.

There is a need for more options, not less or none, for individuals to choose Medicare advantage plans. The government should be working with the private sector (health insurance companies) in making it more attractive for individuals to obtain these plans. As stated earlier, when government has less control, there is less inefficiency and waste and healthcare costs are decreased.

Chapter 18

Health Insurance Exchange

A health insurance exchange is a set of healthcare plans that individuals may purchase. These plans would be state regulated and subsidized by the federal government and are intended to create a more competitive market for health insurance. The purpose of these exchanges is to offer the consumer more choices of health plans and more competition with the pricing of a healthcare plan. The goal is to have more transparency and accountability since the exchanges are not themselves insurers. The exchanges will offer individuals a choice of private healthcare insurance plans. President Obama and Congress wanted the health insurance exchanges to have a public option, but fortunately, this public health insurance option was dropped from the health reform legislation. If there was a public option, it would lead to an unfair advantage for the public option since it can use taxpayer money and not have the cost restraints and accountability that a private health insurance company must follow. So now, fortunately, in the United States, health insurance exchanges are exclusively from private insurers.

These health insurance exchanges would allow more portability of coverage for an individual in case he/she moved from job to job. These exchanges would help individuals who do not have access to an employer-sponsored insurance plan. The exchanges would have competitive premium rates because of the number of individuals on the various health plans. This would eliminate the disadvantage of trying to get insurance as an individual.

Generally, big corporations can get better health insurance rates because of the number of employees they can add to a particular health insurance plan. They can negotiate for discounted/better rates for their employees. With the health insurance exchange, this would help eliminate that advantage, and each individual can get the same rate as another working in a big company or corporation.

I believe that as part of the solution to the overall healthcare issue, these health insurance exchanges should become a state function with some federal oversight since there would be some federal subsidy. Most of the oversight should be in the states' hands.

Chapter 19

Medicaid–State Responsibility, Not Federal

The federal government matches state Medicaid spending from 50 to 83 percent. Since the federal government is paying a major portion of the bill, this provides a state with an incentive to expand the program. This federal government support of Medicaid allows a state to spend more money than it otherwise would. There is a need for a gradual transfer of Medicaid responsibility to the states. Block grants can be given to the states. This will provide an incentive for the state to control program costs. The states now will have to find and try more innovative ways of providing health insurance to its poor.

Each state should be allowed to organize its Medicaid system according to its needs and priorities. Again, keeping the money and decisions more on a local and state level will eliminate some of the bureaucratic waste and inefficiency and, therefore, decrease overall healthcare costs in our country.

Chapter 20

Tax Benefits for Health Insurance

Government is supposed to work for us. If we are truly a country that wants healthcare coverage for everyone and wants to continue with the excellent quality of care that we currently have, the government should pass laws that will allow more appropriate tax benefits for individuals wanting healthcare for themselves and their families. The real question is do we want to give the government more tax money so that it can have control over our healthcare decisions and over the choices and options we have for healthcare coverage? Also, do we really believe that the government will spend our money more efficiently and wisely then we would?

Therefore, I propose the tax deductions for healthcare spending be more advantageous for the individual rather than for the employer. This would allow insurance to be purchased across state lines. The individual and family can then choose a healthcare plan that is more suitable for them without having to take the one the employer offers. The employer will naturally try to get the best deal possible for his/her company with respect to healthcare coverage. This may be suitable for some of the employees but would not be suitable for all of them. By allowing individuals to buy their own healthcare plan and to allow it to be portable and obtainable across state lines will only make the industry of healthcare more competitive and thereby help to decrease costs and health premiums in the long run.

Tax benefits should also benefit those individuals that purchase health savings accounts and Medicare savings accounts because these individuals will be better informed about healthcare costs and more knowledgeable about health in general. The incentives to spend less money on healthcare and remain healthy with these health/Medicare savings accounts will result in decreasing some of the burden of healthcare costs to the system.

Chapter 21

State Experiments

Individual states should have flexibility in trying different solutions for healthcare that they feel will best meet the needs of their residents. Individual states can then be in a better position to make adjustments if unforeseen problems occur. It is much easier to change laws on the state level than it would ever be on the federal level.

In 2006, Massachusetts passed healthcare reform on a state level in order to try to insure more people living in the state. This was done partially because many Massachusetts' residents who were uninsured utilized emergency rooms as a source of primary care. This caused mounting expenses due to unpaid bills by the uninsured.

In 1986, Congress passed an act called the Emergency Medical Treatment and Active Labor Act (EMTALA). This act required hospitals and emergency services to care for anyone needing emergency treatment regardless of citizenship or legal status or ability to pay. There are many who, as a result, use the emergency room as a free clinic. This adds to the costs of healthcare. Therefore, the Massachusetts healthcare reform was an attempt to solve this problem and to provide health insurance to more of its residents.

Within a short time, Massachusetts has already learned some painful lessons. The main lesson learned is that the actual healthcare costs were significantly higher than the projected healthcare costs. In less than four years, the cost of the state insurance program increased by $600 million, or 42 percent. Even though Massachusetts was able to decrease the percentage of its uninsured population from over 6 percent to less than 3 percent, this came at a substantial price. Benefit cuts will need to be made, and policy changes will need to be constructed, in order to sustain its viability in the future. Therefore, like all well-intended programs initiated by bureaucrats and politicians, the reform plan became exorbitant and the notion that a publicly-run Massachusetts plan could control cost was not validated.

Other problems with the Massachusetts healthcare reform included too large a subsidy to low- and medium-income earners. Income redistribution usually does not work well. Also, the health insurance exchanges rewarded people for working less and earning less. This is counterproductive and obviously more costly. An additional problem included mandates with employers' insurance plans. This will weaken a company's incentive for providing coverage for its employees, and the company will either choose to pay a fine or allow the employee to go into the subsidized state-run exchanges.

Hopefully Massachusetts will learn that by passing legislation that makes it harder for employers and employees to obtain health insurance and easier to go into a subsidize plan by the government, it will drive the costs of healthcare in the wrong direction and become more costly for everyone who has to foot the bill.

Over time, I believe that states will be in a better position to correct their errors in providing healthcare to its residents since they are subject to a balanced budget and cannot go over a budget in a fiscal year. Although, there is an understandable fear that the federal government would bail out states (especially those states that voted for the president) if they went over budget, just like the government bailed out General Motors and Chrysler and many of the nations' banks.

We all know how successful and inexpensive it was to bailout the automobile companies and banks.

By allowing experimentation by the states to control their healthcare costs, other states can learn from another state's errors and hopefully not repeat them. This is how medicine is practiced. Experiments are done to answer a question by different groups of scientist and when the results are valid and reproducible, the right approach for a treatment is found. This benefits everyone, and even though some of the experiments may have failed to have a favorable outcome, the best approach was eventually discovered.

Chapter 22

Doctor Regulation

There needs to be less regulation on doctors/providers. When there are such onerous regulations, there is more time taken away from actual patient care. Most of the regulations were enacted by bureaucrats or lawyers or politicians whose jobs involved a lot of paperwork. When a physician or provider has to do a lot of paperwork, it usually is unnecessary or repetitive. For example, there is a need to document and describe a particular problem in a patient's records such as chest pain. Even though this is done adequately in the record and a licensed physician or provider has determined a need to order a stress test to investigate this chest pain, usually more forms need to be completed to justify ordering the test. Also, there is a possibility that a nurse or a physician from an insurance company needs to talk to the doctor/provider who ordered the test and review the reasoning why a certain test was ordered. This duplication and triplication of a service only frustrates the doctor/provider and does not help the patient.

Also, the regulations and laws should be simplified so that they can be understood clearly by both physicians/providers and patients. As stated in a previous book, there is a need to endorse "simplification attorneys," a new law practice that simplifies legislation so that all Americans can understand. Most of the regulations and laws are so ambiguous and complicated that many attorneys cannot understand them, let alone the average American citizen.

The regulations should involve more oversight and not control or duplication of services or work. Doctors and providers are always responsible for every encounter they have with a patient. If they had to document and justify decisions they make in several formats and on several forms or with several reviewers, not only would this be a waste of time, it would be a disservice to the profession and to the people that they treat.

In exchange for decreasing regulations and paperwork, physicians can practice under a free market system, where their fees can be posted on the Internet so that patients can make better-informed decisions about the costs of their services and if they should go elsewhere for a similar service.

Also there should be national/federal licensing for physicians and not state licensing. All too often, a physician that was reprimanded in one state moves to another state and continues his or her bad behavior. This would help protect the public more from some of the "bad" doctors. However, I believe that state agencies are better at oversight of physicians than a federal agency. Therefore, the licensing of a physician can be national and a physician can practice in all fifty states, but the oversight of doctors'/providers' activities can be done at the state level. The doctor or provider would have to pay a federal fee for his or her license and a state fee for the oversight.

Chapter 23

Pharmaceutical Companies

The food drug administration (FDA) needs to be overhauled. The FDA makes it harder for pharmaceutical companies to develop new drugs on the market because of all the regulations. These new drugs are more costly and slower to develop because of these regulations. There is a need to remove the hurdles so that newer drugs can be utilized by the public quicker, so that they may benefit from them. For example, many drugs take eight to twelve years after they are developed to be available to the public. Sometimes an unintended side effect causes the medication to be removed completely. This is especially absurd when dealing with antibiotics or cancer medications, since the benefits usually would outweigh the risk and any harm from the potential unintended side effects. If aspirin needed to be approved today by the FDA, many believe it would never be approved for public consumption.

Also, as stated earlier with tort reform, there needs to be less liability when the public is informed of potential side effects, and then encounters those side effects. There is always a statistical risk or chance of a side effect with any medication. When someone has a side effect that can be expected in a certain percentage of patients, there should not be liability for the pharmaceutical company or for the doctor/provider that prescribed the medication. The liability issue is more pertinent or appropriate when a company knows of a side effect and doesn't disclose it or covers it up.

One of the issues affecting the costs of healthcare is the cost of medications. I propose that medications can be bought by any American resident with any pharmaceutical outfit in the world. Many times, Americans can get their medications more inexpensively from Canada or Mexico via the Internet. If an American resident has a valid doctor's or provider's prescription, he or she should be able to obtain the medication abroad if it is affordable to him/her. The individual will need to sign a liability waiver when he/she purchases medications from outside the United States, where it is most likely less regulated. The individual will understand that he/she is making an informed choice to purchase medication more cheaply but without the usual legal protection. This will drive down the costs of many medications by adding competition and creating a global market for medications.

Chapter 24

Immigration

If there is going to be any meaningful comprehensive healthcare reform involving increasing the number of people living in the United States who have healthcare coverage, then the illegal immigration issue must be addressed. Because of EMTALA, a Congressional act in 1986 where emergency rooms and hospitals must provide care regardless of citizenship, legal status, or ability to pay, hospitals and emergency rooms and the physicians who care for these individuals absorb the costs without any compensation. This puts a burden on healthcare costs and increases the cost of private insurance, which is passed on to the consumers who purchase healthcare insurance. Therefore, it is cost effective in the long run to address this issue. Not to mention, it is more humane to propose an avenue where illegal immigrants can become legal immigrants and eventually citizens of this great nation.

I am proposing an immigration bill that will eventually allow illegal immigrants to become American citizens. The bill will be outlined as follows:

a) All illegal immigrants must register within 180 days of the passage of the immigration bill.

b) Registration will consist of issuing a type of immigration card, similar to a driver's license, which will include the name, current address, date the card was issued, and a picture.

c) Ten years of US residency must elapse after the date the card was issued, before one can apply for citizenship. The reasoning for choosing ten years of residency is that legal immigrants can apply for citizenship after five years of residency.

d) There will be yearly fees in addition to regular taxes for one to be eligible for US citizenship. The fees will be applied as follows. These fees will depend on income earned the previous calendar year.
- For incomes less than $25,000, the fee would be $1000 per year.

- For incomes between $25,000 and $50,000, the fee would be $1500 per year.
- For incomes over $50,000, the fee would be $2000 per year.

e) With the immigration card (IM), one would have the legal right to reside in the United States, be included in the census, and not have to worry about deportation. Also, the IM card would entitle a holder to obtain healthcare benefits in the United States.

The IM card would be invalidated if one were convicted of a felony. An immigrant would be deported after serving a sentence. If the offender had children, who are citizens of the United States, the offender must still be deported, but the children could remain in the United States. The offender would have the time to appeal his or her felony while he/she is serving prison time in our country.

f) After the passage of this immigration bill, the only entry into the United States would be by current legal means, which is the avenue that legal immigrants presently use to become US citizens over time.

Of course, for illegal immigrants to become US citizens and to stop illegal immigration, our country needs to secure its borders. Therefore, if we are serious about containing the costs of healthcare and providing insurance for the residents of the United States, we need to tackle the issue of illegal immigration both responsibly and fairly. Our nation has become a great nation because of the contributions of legal immigrants over the centuries. It is time to begin a process giving all residents of the United States an opportunity to become legal citizens. If illegal immigrants wish to remain in our country and become legal, they will need to prove that by paying yearly fees as outlined in d) above. They will need to not commit a felony in our country. We are a nation of laws and should remain a nation of laws. As a nation, we need to set an example for our children and grandchildren that we can be compassionate and can allow those who have lived here for years to become citizens, even though they entered illegally. However, the process of becoming a US citizen needs to be a fair one, especially since many immigrants came here legally, followed all the rules, and made tremendous sacrifices just to have an opportunity to be a citizen in our country. Also, as a nation of laws, we need to enforce the existing laws and make securing our borders a priority.

Chapter 25

Reform Other Entitlements

Entitlements account for over half of federal spending, and it is said that they are untouchable. That line of reasoning is completely absurd and illogical. Families have to contain costs and try to keep within their budget. If they decide that where they live cannot be changed and their mortgage accounts for over half of their budget, they have little else for other necessities, including utilities, food, clothing, transportation, education, and entertainment. So if they wish to have more expendable money, they can choose to move to a home that has lower mortgage payments where they would have more to spend on other items. It is completely foolish to think that a family cannot move when that option exists. Likewise, the government cannot think that entitlements are a guaranteed right that can never change. Adjustments will need to be made in order to keep these entitlements solvent in the future.

Medicare is a government entitlement that was addressed in Chapter 13 of Section II. Just as there is a need for changing the entry age with Medicare, that same need applies to those receiving Social Security benefits. The average life expectancy increased by over seven years since 1966 when Medicare was enacted, and by sixteen years since 1935, when the Social Security act was passed. Therefore, at the time social security was passed, the entry age was sixty-five and the average life expectancy was sixty-two which is three years less than the entry age. Hence, it was not anticipated that such a high percentage of the population would be living over the age of sixty-five. If we were to use the same logic today as in 1935, Social Security entry age today would begin at eighty-one, which is three years of age more than the average life expectancy today. Obviously, we as a nation cannot jump up to an entry age of eighty-one for Social Security. But, we can begin a gradual increase to an entry age of seventy.

This increase in the Social Security entry age will only affect those under the age of fifty-five. Beginning in 2013, the entry age would increase one year every two years. That is, for those born after 1958, the entry age would be sixty-six. For those born after 1960, the entry age would be sixty-seven. For those born after 1962 the entry age would be sixty-eight. For those born after 1964, the entry age would be sixty-nine. Like the entry age previously proposed for Medicare, for all Americans born after December 31, 1966, the entry age for Social Security would be seventy.

There also needs to be flexibility in allowing individual localities such as counties or cities to reform Social Security in the manner they consider most beneficial for the people living in their county or city or town. For example, Galveston, Texas, is an example where the private alternative for Social Security has been successful. In 1981, employees of Galveston County and two other counties in Texas (Brazoria and Matagorda) voted by a 78 to 22 percent margin to opt out of the government run Social Security program. In 1983, Congress voted to eliminate localities from choosing to opt out of Social Security.

Since that time, the private model utilized in Galveston by the employees of the county, more than doubled their investment for most workers when compared to the government Social Security program. So obviously, a private sector option to Social Security needs to be allowed at the local level, since it is more likely than the government to be fiscally responsible. In Galveston, the plan was a voluntary one and over two-thirds of the government employees in the county chose to participate in the private plan. The other employees remained on the regular Social Security program.

There are differences between the Galveston plan and Social Security. Both plans have mandatory participation and the amount contributed by the employee and employer is similar. Some of the differences include no retirement age with the Galveston plan. Presently, Social Security retirement age is sixty-five years. With Social Security, if one works after the age of sixty-five, the benefits are reduced. The Galveston plan does not reduce the benefits if one continues to work after the age of sixty-five. Galveston employees are to designate their beneficiary so that the benefits they have accrued go to the family member that they desire. Whereas Social Security has "default" beneficiaries, which may include divorced spouses.

Social Security does have an advantage in that there is inflation adjustment, but even with the inflation adjustment, its total benefit was still much less than the private plan. The private plan also does not offer additional benefits to spouses, as does Social Security, but in the private Galveston plan, the individual has more control over what happens to the benefits when he or she dies.

The biggest distinction between Social Security and the Galveston private plan is that the private plan puts the individual participant in charge and not the government. As stated many times earlier in the book, when the individual has more at stake, he or she will be more accountable and fiscally responsible and, therefore, less inefficient and wasteful. Our government does not do a good job as a nanny state. The bigger government gets, the less efficient it runs, and the more risks there will be for our children and grandchildren to be unfairly burdened with unsustainable debts to pay.

Medicaid should eventually be the states' responsibility, as outlined in Chapter 19 of Section II. This is a step in the right direction toward fiscal responsibility involving entitlements.

The United States currently pays about $20 billion to farmers each year in direct subsidies. Many of these subsidies are provided without regard to the economic need or the financial condition of the recipient. Corn is the top crop receiving subsidy payments. The subsidies are further enhanced by regulations requiring ethanol being blended into fuel. What results is a direct transfer of income from the general taxpayer to selected farm owners. There is an immediate need for Congress to take a closer look at this and eliminate many of the farm subsidies that are unnecessary. Right now, the federal government micromanages the agricultural sector, and this creates less efficient planting and induces more borrowing by farmers, and results in less market innovation. The more the government is involved with handing out our taxpayer money to the agricultural sector, the more overall damage there is to our economy. Also, when the federal government subsidizes programs, there are more bureaucratic inefficiencies and fraud, and more scandal with politicians in Congress using the distribution of these payments for political gain. The government accountability office found that $500 million in farm subsidies are paid improperly or fraudulently each year.

With respect to farm subsidies, it is felt that they damaged US trade relations. The World Trade Center Organization estimated that if there was a one third drop in all tariffs around the world, global output would increase and the United States would benefit by $164 billion. But the United States farm subsidies and protections are in the way.

Therefore, it is time for politicians to do the right thing and address untouchable entitlements and make the necessary changes to keep it viable in the future. Some programs will need to be cut drastically, such as farm subsidies. Other programs such as Medicare and Social Security will need to change their entry age. Also Medicaid should become the responsibility of the states and become more localized and, therefore, fiscally more accountable and responsible. Only in this way, can we make the necessary sacrifices and stop "living for today" by borrowing money for our current needs at the expense of our country's future.

Chapter 26

Funding for Abortion

When the healthcare reform bill was being discussed and debated, a majority of Americans favored banning any abortion funding in the bill. In fact, a group of Democrats led by Congressman Stupak stated they would not support a healthcare reform bill that funded abortion. However, when Scott Brown won the Senate seat in Massachusetts previously held by Ted Kennedy, the Democratic controlled Congress was forced to use the Senate version of the healthcare reform bill in order to ensure its passage. This was done so that the Senate version of the bill adopted prior to Scott Brown's election in January 2010 could not be changed or amended if it did return to the Senate for a vote. Congressman Stupak and his group of Democrats who were not in favor of federal funding of abortion ended up, in March of 2010, voting for the Senate version of the healthcare bill after being given assurances with an executive order signed by President Obama. This executive order stated that federal funding of abortion would not occur. This is, however, untrue and misleading.

·The healthcare reform bill did authorize money for services at community health centers, and these community health centers can use the funds as they see fit. This means they can be used directly for elective abortions. Also, the bill will allow states to set up public insurance plans and, even though the money will not directly cover abortions, it will cover reproductive services. Depending on how a state chooses to define reproductive services, there could be funding at the state level for abortions.

It is unfair that the majority of Americans' will is ignored. Private organizations can help fund abortions if they choose to do so. The indigent can still obtain medical coverage if she qualifies for Medicaid and will not have to pay for her abortions. As a physician and a person of faith, I have a strong pro-life point of view. In my career, I have spoken to many women who have regretted having had an abortion. Abortion is a personal issue and is legal in our country, and should be available for all Americans who choose to have an abortion. However, a minority viewpoint should not force the majority, who do not believe there should be federal funding for abortion, to help pay for something they believe is morally wrong.

Chapter 27

Education

The government can be very helpful in the healthcare arena by investing in the education of Americans. It did a very good job educating Americans about the dangers of smoking. Because of that antismoking campaign, many young people put pressure on their parents, who had been smoking since their teenage years, to quit smoking. The same type of nationwide campaign needs to be done on various aspects of healthcare. For instance, back in the early 1960s, President Kennedy launched a national campaign for young Americans in school to get more exercise. I remember in Catholic school having to take various physical tests, such as how many sit ups or pushups or pull-ups can be done in a minute. The health of our nation would benefit if there was more education and exercise in the early school years. Just as we now learn mathematics, science, English grammar, reading, and writing at a young age, students can have classes on health that educate and inform them about nutrition, diet, exercise, and health maintenance. There needs to be a greater emphasis on health in our schools.

More Americans need to learn at a young age about the dangers of certain lifestyle habits such as smoking, overeating, drugs, and so on. This way, they can learn to respect their body in both physical and mental ways. They may make healthier choices when they have more knowledge and education.

Having Americans become better educated with their health and with other healthcare issues will result in more productive citizens, who will more than likely become contributors to our society and help keep this nation great.

Section III

Congress and the Presidency

Chapter 28

What Is Congress' Role?

The best case scenario would be to repeal Obamacare. This would give us the best chance to do it right and improve the healthcare system with more responsible solutions and cost containing measures. However even with the Republicans winning the majority in the House of Representatives in 2010, most likely the repeal will not pass in the Senate, and even if portions of the repeal law pass in the Senate, President Obama will invariably veto it.

Therefore, at this time, the strategy would be to limit its effect by holding the spending allocated for new bureaucratic agencies. This will need to be done by Hal Rogers, a congressman from Kentucky, who is the committee chairman of the appropriations committee. This committee is in charge of the specific expenditures of money by the government. It is very hard for our government to eliminate an agency once it has been created and the best way of avoiding unnecessary expenses with more waste and fraud is by stopping the agencies from being created in the first place.

Our Congress needs to show support for the continued battle by the states challenging the constitutionality of the forced insurance mandate. It is obviously unconstitutional to force individuals to buy a service if they choose not to buy it. Over twenty states have challenged the constitutionality of the healthcare reform bill of 2010 and Florida and Virginia have already had success. In Virginia, the insurance mandate provision was deemed unconstitutional and in Florida, the entire bill was seen as unconstitutional. This battle will undoubtedly reach the Supreme Court, where four of its liberal members will most likely adjudicate the issue on political grounds and try to legislate from the bench. There are four members of the bench that are constitutionalists (that is, they believe in the constitution as a document that defines our inalienable rights and not one that can be reshaped or reformed) and will undoubtedly find the Insurance mandate portion of the bill unconstitutional. This will most likely result in Judge Kennedy being the deciding vote on an issue of this magnitude. Hopefully, he will base his decision on the constitution. Even if the Supreme Court rules in favor of declaring the insurance mandate unconstitutional, the repeal of the 2010 healthcare reform bill cannot be enforced until there is a new President in the White House.

Chapter 29

Winning Strategy

The strategy for Republicans to win the Congressional and Presidential elections should begin now by:

a) Working to maintain the majority in the House of Representatives, and since more democratic senatorial seats are in play in the elections of 2012, the republicans have a good chance of obtaining a majority in the Senate

b) Putting forward solutions (prior to the 2012 elections) for the healthcare bill once the bill is repealed

These solutions were outlined in the previous section. Legislation for tort reform, allowing insurance across state lines, keeping the no exclusion provision for pre-existing conditions, and the cap for catastrophic care should be passed by the House of Representatives prior to the 2012 elections. The Democratic senators can then go on record if they choose not to support these measures, and for some of them up for reelection in 2012, this can be a referendum on their reelection bid. Also, if any of these bills make it to the White House, President Obama can veto them. This can be a referendum for the 2012 presidential election. There will be a clear distinction for the voters as to whether they want to reelect a president who supports Obamacare, which will be ineffective and costly, with increased government employees and government control over our lives, or vote for a candidate that believes in less government control and that the private sector has better solutions and is more in line with the goals and intentions of our founding fathers.

c) Comprising a dream team of candidates to serve in the White House so that an individual isn't the solution to our country's problems, but rather a team of experienced and capable/qualified individuals is (This dream team is outlined in the Appendix.)

d) Have the candidate who wins the Republican nomination for the presidency in 2012 pledge the following ten things:

- <u>Smaller Government</u>. There are now over three million federal government workers and there is significant duplication of services and inefficiency. A pledge should be made to decrease the size of the federal government and to eliminate departments that are either duplicate or inefficient.

- Fewer Taxes. Besides decreasing corporate taxes to stimulate businesses in the private sector and eliminating the death tax for individuals, there needs to be a significant push to reform the tax code. Either the fair tax or the flat tax would be a significant improvement over our current tax code system, which allows politicians to use the tax code for personal gain or their party's benefit. I prefer the fair tax, but believe that the flat tax is an easier transition at this point in history.

- Support Capitalism and the Private Sector. They create the jobs in America that improve our economy. Government control and expansion is not the solution for unemployment, and going toward a more socialist state is part of the problem, resulting in more financial unrest and even more unemployment.

- Not Increase the National Debt. Our children and grandchildren do not deserve to be riddled with debt that accumulated because we were afraid to act fiscally responsible and control our expenses. A balanced budget amendment or pay-as-you-go strategy needs to be enforced in order for Congress to stop being tempted to borrow more money for its pet projects.

- Protect our Borders. In order to maintain a safer nation, our Borders must be protected so that there is less likelihood of terrorist infiltration on our homeland. Also, the immigration issue and reform can be addressed properly *after* our borders are protected.

- Not Appease Our Enemies. For a stronger National Defense, our nation needs to be consistent in our defense of our values, including individual and human rights. We should not be naïve in believing that having a dialogue with dictators will accomplish peace. We should not react to foreign events in the world, but already know in advance how to respond because of our core values and beliefs.

- Vow to Repeal Obamacare. Replace Obamacare with solutions that work for the majority of Americans and allow healthcare to be strong and sustainable in the future.

- Treat All Citizens Equally. Promise not to engage in class or race or gender warfare. Decisions will be made to benefit Americans not just a class or race or gender, and so on.

- <u>Seek Term Limits for Congress.</u> Since most politicians over time will want to stay in power, they will spend more time trying to get reelected than actually serving the people. Therefore, I propose that an individual cannot serve more than twelve years in Congress in his or her lifetime. This could be two Senate terms or one Senate term and three terms in the House of Representatives, or six terms in the House of Representatives.
- <u>Civility.</u> A standard needs to be set that is the same for everyone. There should be no character assassination or name calling if one disagrees with another's position. Also, misdeeds done by politicians should be dealt with swiftly and in the same manner, and not be dependent on party affiliation or which party is in power.

Conclusion

Americans have a choice between having individual control over their healthcare or allowing big government to decide what is good for them. The 2012 presidential election is a window of opportunity to correct a wrong. However well-intentioned Obamacare was meant to be, if left as it is with a massive bureaucracy, the citizens of this country will suffer. In my opinion, Obamacare, by 2020, will result in tens of thousands of premature deaths a year, which is a much higher number than the number of American deaths resulting from 9/11 and the casualties from two wars fighting terrorism over the last decade.

The solutions need to be comprehensive and flexible. More doctors/providers need to be involved in the decision-making process, not politicians or lobbyists with their special interests. When a portion of a new healthcare bill is not working, it will need to be changed. In medicine, this is done all the time. Physicians do not continue therapy that is shown to be counterproductive, but rather try a different method and change strategies.

All sectors of our economy including the debt, budget, defense, entitlements, and non-discretionary spending will need to be addressed. The public needs to be educated and informed of the real dangers of continuing to spend recklessly and not addressing our national debt. Just as the average citizen has to do in his or her household, fiscal responsibility is essential. The average citizen cannot afford huge interest payments and debts. He/she learns to curtail spending and spend within his/her means. The US Government should do the same.

The immigration issue needs to be addressed so that all residents in our country can be treated fairly and equally. Immigration should not be used as a political issue in order to obtain more votes and remain in power.

Obamacare needs to be repealed. The Republican Party needs to begin a strategy to win the White House in 2012 by promising to repeal Obamacare and slowly change and improve our healthcare system with solutions included in this book and other solutions that are deemed to have a good chance of success. The changes will need to apply equally to everyone, and there should be no exceptions or waivers made for companies or organizations that are favorites/allies of a political party.

The politicians need to know what real people want. They need to get off their high horse and stop acting like elitists or a ruling class by behaving as if they (the government) know better what is good for the individual. Individuals know better what is best for them, not the politicians.

Americans need to understand that this is a time for sacrifice and not accept the bull that government has the solutions or the answers to our problems. We will be a healthier nation if we take more personal responsibility and become more educated on healthcare issues, and allow the healthcare needs to be between a physician/provider and a patient. Americans also have to hold the politicians accountable for making the tough choices in decreasing spending and make them understand that they will not be reelected if they do not do their job and fulfill their promises. By demanding that government become smaller and have less control over our lives, we as Americans will have more freedom and liberty and individual choice, as our forefathers had always intended for this great nation.

Sources

"Enrollment in Medicaid Surges to 48M, a Record Share of US Population," *Arizona Daily Star,* October 1, 2010, accessed February 6, 2011, http://azstarnet.com/news/national/article_9235dc42-ddc6-563f-b2e6-f15e35eacdc9.html?mode=story.

Beck, Glenn, *Broke: The Plan to Restore Our Trust, Truth and Treasure* (New York: Simon & Schuster, Inc., 2010), 193-213.

Cassedy, James, *Medicine in America: A Short History* (Baltimore, MD: The Johns Hopkins University Press, 1991), 3-8, 155-158.

Crosta, Peter, "Study Of 31 Countries Finds Wide Variations In Cancer Survival Rates," *Medical News Today,* July 18, 2008, accessed December 11, 2010, http://www.medicalnewstoday.com /articles/115086.php.

Edwards, Chris, "Agricultural Subsidies," *Cato Institute,* June 2009, accessed February 12, 2011, http://www.downsizinggovernment.org /agriculture/subsidies.

Edwards, Chris, *Downsizing the Federal Government* (Washington, DC: Cato Institute, 2005), 51-78 (Kindle Edition).

Galewitz, Phil, "The Debate over Selling Insurance across State Lines," *Kaiser Health News*, February 3, 2010, accessed January 22, 2011, http://www.kaiserhealthnews.org/Stories/2009/Novembe r/06/health-insurance-across-state-lines.aspx.

HealthCare.Gov, "At Risk: Pre-Existing Conditions Could Affect 1 in 2 Americans," accessed January 23, 2011, http://www.healthcare.gov/center/reports/preexisting.html.

Hogan, Lunney, Gabel, and Joanne Lynn, "Medicare Beneficiaries' Costs of Care in the Last Year of Life," *Health Affairs,* July-August, 2001, accessed February 6, 2011, http://content.healthaffairs.org/content/20/4/188.full.

Holbrook, Ray, and Alcestis Oberg, "Galveston County: A Model for Social Security Reform," *National Center for Policy Analysis,* April 26, 2005, accessed February 12, 2011, http://www.ncpa.org/pub/ba514.

Kaiser Family Foundation, "Explaining Health Care Reform," accessed January 30, 2011, http://www.kff.org/healthreform/upload/7908.pdf.

Krupa, Carolyne, "By Late Career, 61% of Doctors Have Been Sued," *American Medical News* (53) 16, 2010: 1-2.

Mattive, Nilus, "Galveston vs. Social Security," *Money and Markets,* July 13, 2010, accessed February 12, 2011, http://www.moneyand markets.com/galveston-vs-social-security-39613.

Nano, Stephanie, "Study: Malpractice Worries Help Drive Health Costs," *Associate Press*, April 13, 2010, accessed December 19, 2010, http://www.google.com/hostednews/ap/article/ALeqM5g1X8n7Ct5xyKui-jeaw4JVS8AXYwD9F2DTP81.

Perry, Rick, *Fed Up! Our Fight to Save America from Washington* (New York: Little, Brown and Company, 2010), 75-94 (Kindle Edition).

Reuters, "US Life Expectancy Hits a New High of 78," accessed January 29, 2011, http://www.reuters.com/article/2009/08/20/us-usa-lifespan-idUSTRE57I6BF20090820.

Rizo, Chris, "California's Landmark Med-Mal Law Called a National Model," *LegalNewsline.com*, October 14, 2009, accessed December 18, 2010, http://www.legalnewsline.com/spotlight/223419-californias-landmark-med-mal-law-called-a-national-model.

Rizo, Chris, "Texas Legal Environment Improves, Survey Shows," *The Southeast Texas Record,* March 22, 2010, accessed December 19, 2010. http://www.setexasrecord.com/news/225475-texas-legal-environment-improves-survey-shows.

Rutkow, Ira, *Seeking the Cure: A History of Medicine in America* (New York, NY: Scribner, 2010), 1-4.

Sack, Kevin, "Arizona's Medicaid Cuts a Sure Sign of the Financial Times," *Starnews,* December 5, 2010, Section A, Final Edition.

Sorrel, Amy Lynn, "Texas Liability Reforms Spur Plunge in Premiums and Law Suits" *amednews.com*, September 8, 2008, accessed December 18, 2010, http://www.ama-assn.org/amednews/2008/09/08/prl20908.htm.

Tully, Shawn, "5 Painful Health-Care Lessons from Massachusetts," *Fortune,* June 16, 2010, accessed February 6, 2011, http://money.cnn.com/2010/06/15/news/economy/massachusetts_healthcare_reform.fortune/index.htm.

Appendix

The dream team should consist of a group of prominent Republicans who have experience and capability. It would not matter who the Republicans nominate to run for president in 2012 because they would all share the same goals and principles outlined in Chapter 29.

Dept. of State-Jeb Bush

Dept. of Treasury-Paul Ryan

Dept. of Defense-David Petraeus

Dept. of Justice-Rudy Giuliani or National Security Adviser

Dept. of Interior-Mitt Romney or Chairman of Council of Economics

Dept. of Agriculture-Haley Barbour

Dept. of Commerce-Mike Pence

Dept. of Labor-Chris Christie

Dept. of Health and Human Services-Bill Frist

Dept. of Housing and Urban Development-Donald Trump

Dept. of Transportation-Eric Cantor

Dept. of Energy-Sarah Palin

Dept. of Education-Mike Huckabee

Dept. of Veterans Affairs-John McCain

Dept. of Homeland Security-Michelle Bachmann

Presidential Advisers- Herman Cain, Mitch Daniels, Jim DeMint, Newt Gingrich, Darrell Issa, Bobby Jindal, Ron Paul, Tim Pawlenty, Rick Perry, Rick Santorum and John Thune.

VP- ???

President- ???

Of course there are many more qualified Republicans and individuals who could be included on this dream team, but the point is for the Republican Party to be united in winning the presidency in 2012 and bringing America and its health back in the right direction.

Made in the USA
San Bernardino, CA
31 January 2013